Play the Electronic Keyboard
Book 1

Nicholas Haines

2.50

By the same author
Play the Electronic Keyboard Book 2
Composing at the Electronic Keyboard Books 1 and 2
Tunes for Electronic Keyboard Books 1 and 2

LONGMAN GROUP UK LIMITED
Longman House
Burnt Mill, Harlow, Essex CM20 2JE, England
and Associated Companies throughout the world

First published 1986
Fifth impression 1990

ISBN 0-582-22460-8

Set in 11/13 pt Helvetica Regular (Lasercomp).

Produced by Longman Group (FE) Ltd
Printed in Hong Kong

Contents

Introduction   page 4
The portable keyboard

Unit 1 The instrument section and   6
some keyboard effects
Sustain
Vibrato
Keyboard exercises

Unit 2 The rhythm section (1)   8
Tempo control
Keyboard rhythm exercises

Unit 3 The rhythm section (2)   10
Tempo light
The fill-in button
Rhythm exercises

Unit 4 The auto-bass and chord   13
section
C and G chords, swing rhythm
C, F and G chords, latin rhythm

Unit 5 Note values   16
Time signatures
Repeat signs
Rhythms and notes
Waltz and rock rhythms

Unit 6 Finding the notes   20
Musical alphabet, Scrabble
Twinkle, Twinkle Little Star
Frère Jacques
Unto us is Born a Son
Blue Danube Waltz

Unit 7 Starting to read music   23
Fingering
Note exercises; Sailing, Gliding, Rocking
'Ode to Joy'

Unit 8 Combining melody with chords 27
Some new signs
Up-beat bar
Playing louder and softer
Oh When the Saints go Marching in
'Ode to Joy'

Unit 9 Minor chords and the C major 30
scale
Some new notes
Scales
Note stems
Chord pattern exercise
Canon
The Skaters Waltz
Au Clair de la Lune

Unit 10 Quavers   34
Slurs
Staccato
Two more notes
Rhythm exercises
Cradle Song
The Ash Grove

Unit 11 Dotted crotchets   38
Rests
Rhythm exercises
Michael Row the Boat Ashore
Theme from the 'New World' Symphony

Introduction

The portable keyboard

There are three main sizes of portable keyboard:

1   Micro-mini keyboard

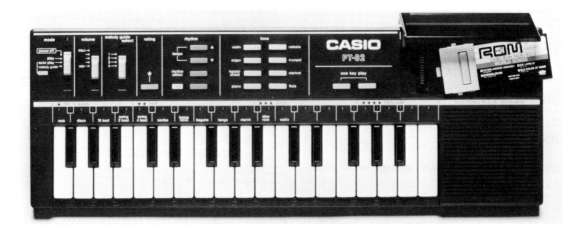

These keyboards often have small buttons to operate the automatic functions. The keys are 'mini size'. It is possible to play only one note at a time (monophonic).

2   Mini keyboard

The range of this keyboard is bigger. To save space, the automatic chord functions 'share' the lower section of the keyboard. Up to eight notes at a time can be played on the main keyboard (polyphonic).

These keyboards have full size keys. They offer a wide range of rhythms and instruments, and can be used as performing instruments.

Getting the best from your portable keyboard

Always use a mains adapter if possible. Although most keyboards have battery provision, this can be wasteful, especially if you forget to switch it off! The keyboard has its own speaker, but you can get a fuller sound if you connect up the output socket (line or aux) to a hi-fi system or a combo-amplifier. You can record the keyboard by connecting the output socket to the tape recorder input.

There is often a pitch control at the back of the keyboard. Check the tuning against a piano or organ. The larger keyboards have a socket so that you can plug in a foot-operated volume control. This is a very useful accessory. Your hands will have enough to do playing the music without adjusting the volume control.

Lastly, always make sure you can easily see the music. If the keyboard does not have its own built-in music-stand, a small desk-stand placed behind the keyboard is probably the best solution.

Getting to know your keyboard

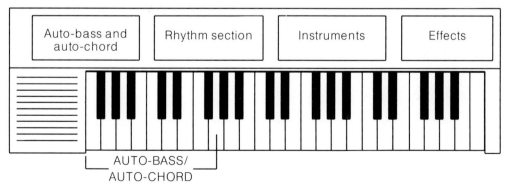

Although every make of keyboard is different, they all have a selection of automatic bass lines, chords, rhythms, and effects. The first few units will help you to understand how the switches, buttons and keys can be used in the best possible way.

UNIT 1
The instrument section and some keyboard effects

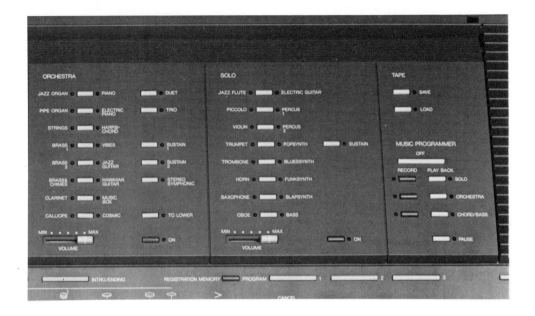

Your keyboard can make the sounds of different instruments. Many of these, such as a violin and cello, you would expect to find in an orchestra. You will naturally find keyboard instruments like the piano and organ. Alongside these traditional instruments, you will find new 'space age' sounds such as 'Synthi Sound', 'Cosmic' and 'Funny Fuzz'.

Some instruments will sound at different pitches. Compare a low instrument, such as a cello or trombone, with a higher one like a flute or glockenspiel. Really get to know what each instrument sounds like so that you will be able to give plenty of variety to every piece of music that you play. Don't stick to the same instrument all the time even if it is your favourite. Remember that the portable keyboard can give you only one instrument at a time, so be prepared to change from one instrument to another.

Sustain

This control makes the sound linger on after you have pressed the key. The sustain effect is used best with percussive sounds like a glockenspiel.

Vibrato

This control adds a wavering effect to the sound of the instrument. Orchestral instruments sound much 'warmer' with the vibrato switch on.

1. Look at all the instruments on the keyboard. Pick out the ones which imitate orchestral instruments. Compare their sounds by experimenting with some of these note patterns. You can play the notes together or separately.

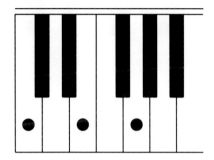 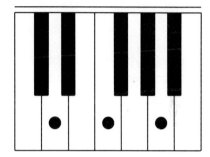

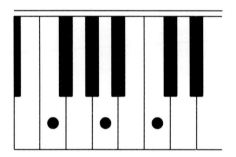 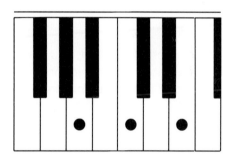

2. Choose a piano sound. With the sustain switch on, run your fingers up and down the white, and then the black notes of the keyboard. Repeat this action but with the sustain switch turned off. Do you hear the difference?
   Can you hear the same effect with the following instruments – organ, chimes, glockenspiel, xylophone, and vibraphone?

3. Choose a violin sound. With the vibrato switch on, press any note for a few seconds. Hear how the wavering effect of the vibrato changes the tone of the instrument. Does the vibrato effect start immediately or does it build up gradually over a few seconds? Try the same with a cello, trumpet, oboe, clarinet, and guitar.

UNIT 2
The rhythm section (1)

Find the rhythm section on the keyboard. Here are some of the most common rhythms found on electronic keyboards today.

Rhythm	Number of beats	Rhythm	Number of beats
Rock	4	Bossa nova	4
Slow rock	4	Tango	4
Rock 'n' roll	4	Rhumba	4
Disco	4	Waltz	3
Swing	4	Jazz waltz	3
Latin	4	March	2/4
Samba	4	Polka	2

At the touch of a button, you can have a drum kit playing along with the melody.

To start the rhythm section, choose any rhythm on the keyboard. Press the start or synchro/start button. The start button will set the auto-rhythm playing immediately. The synchro/start (or touch/start) button will set the tempo light flashing.

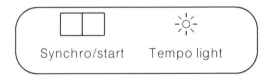

Press any of the keys on the auto-section of the keyboard in order to start the auto-rhythm playing.

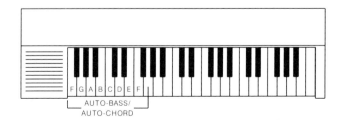

Your hands are now in position to play the melody on the main keyboard.

The rhythm section is really an imitation drum kit. You should be able to hear some of the percussion instruments. For example, a march has a bass drum on the first beat and a snare drum or cymbal on the second beat.

MARCH

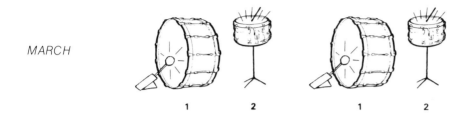

The waltz is the only rhythm with a three-beat pattern so it should be easy to recognize.

WALTZ

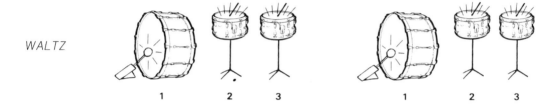

Tempo control

The speed of the rhythm can be altered with the tempo control. To make it easier for you, a number can be given to each mark on the control. These numbers can then be used for the project work throughout the book.

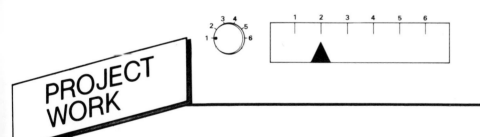

PROJECT WORK

1. Choose one of the rhythms on the keyboard. Set the tempo control at a slow speed. Start the rhythm using the synchro/start button. Can you hear the 'instruments' playing the rhythm? Gradually increase the speed until the control is at the halfway point. Play any note on the keyboard and keep time with the rhythm.

2. Ask your partner to play some of the rhythms and see if you can recognize which ones are being played.

UNIT 3
The rhythm section (2)

The tempo light

The tempo light is very useful to judge the speed of the rhythm. Choose a four-beat rhythm at a slow tempo. Press the synchro/start button and the light will flash at every beat. No rhythm will sound yet.

Press any key on the auto-chord section. The rhythm section will start to play. Notice that the tempo light will now flash only on the first beat of each bar.

The vertical lines are called bar lines and will help you follow the strong beats. The space between two bar lines is called a bar.

A double bar line marks the end of a piece or a section of it. To stop the rhythm at a double bar, simply press the synchro/start button once again.

The fill-in button

Most keyboards have a fill-in button. When the auto-rhythm is playing, press the fill-in button and the 'drummer' will play one bar's solo. This gives variety to the rhythm and should be used at the ends of phrases. If your keyboard has no fill-in button, just ignore the fill-in directions in the project work.

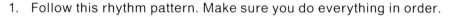

PROJECT WORK

1. Follow this rhythm pattern. Make sure you do everything in order.

   ● Choose a rock rhythm at a moderate tempo.
   ● Press the synchro/start button and the tempo light will flash at every beat.

   ● Press any note on the auto-section of the keyboard. As soon as you do this, the rhythm will start to play.

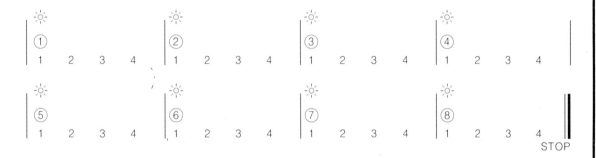

2. Now follow this rhythm pattern, this time with three beats in a bar.

   ● Choose a waltz rhythm at a moderate tempo.
   ● Press the synchro/start button and the tempo light will flash at every beat.

   ● Press any note on the auto-section of the keyboard and the waltz rhythm will start to play.

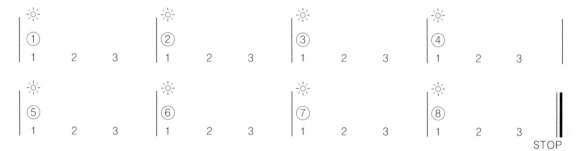

3. Follow this rhythm pattern as you have done in the other two projects, but this time, press the fill-in button at bars 4 and 8. Remember to press the fill-in button *exactly* on the first beat of the bar.

   ● Choose a latin rhythm at a moderate tempo.
   ● Press the synchro/start button, then any note on the auto-section and the latin rhythm will start to play.
   ● On the first beat of bars 4 and 8, press the fill-in button.

①				②				③				④			
1	2	3	4	1	2	3	4	1	2	3	4	FILL-IN			

⑤				⑥				⑦				⑧			
1	2	3	4	1	2	3	4	1	2	3	4	FILL-IN			

STOP

UNIT 4

The auto-bass and chord section

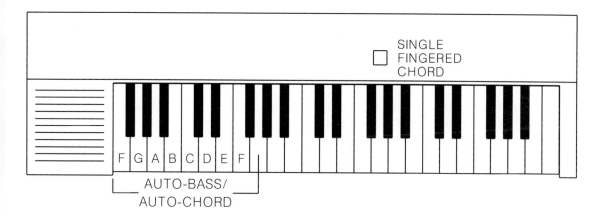

You will see that the keyboard is divided into 2 sections:

1. The main keyboard on which you play the melody.
2. The auto-section on the left of the main keyboard which controls the auto-bass and chords. The micro-mini keyboards have small buttons on the left of the keyboard to control the auto-chords.

To use the auto-bass and chords, press the single fingered chord or auto-chord button. Leave this button pressed down from now on.

What is a chord?

A chord is a group of two or more notes played at the same time.

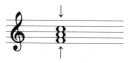

If these notes were not played together, the chord would become a melody.

Chords are really vertical 'props' which
give the melody some kind of support.

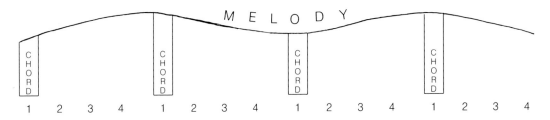

Chords are written down as capital letters
in a square, e.g., C G . Letters written on
their own in a square are called major
chords. Each chord symbol tells you which
key or button to press on the auto-section
of the keyboard. All chord symbols are
shown above each bar and continue to
sound until another chord symbol is
written. There is no need to press the auto-
key again if the bar has no chord marked.
The chord pattern will carry on sounding
until another auto-key is pressed.

Choose a rock rhythm at a moderate
tempo. Press the synchro/start button and
you will be ready to play this four-bar
chord pattern. The chord and rhythm will
sound immediately you press the auto-key.
Make sure you press each auto-key
exactly on the first beat of the bar. Lift your
finger off the auto-key immediately after
you have played the chord.

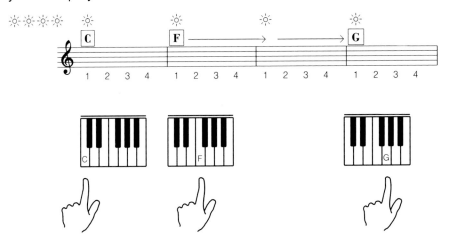

To stop the sound, just press the synchro/
start button once again.

PROJECT WORK

1. You are going to play a two chord pattern using C and G chords.

    ● Choose a swing rhythm at a moderate tempo.
    ● Press the synchro/start button. The chords and rhythm will sound immediately you press the first auto-key.

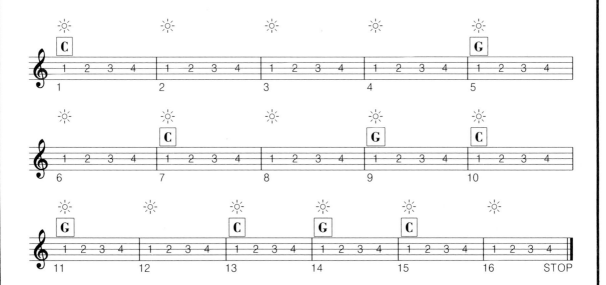

2. There are three chords used in this project: C F and G .

    ● Choose a latin rhythm at a slow tempo.
    ● Press the synchro/start button and you will be ready to play.

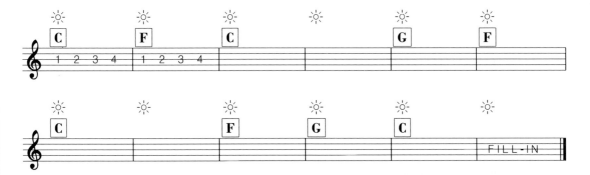

15

UNIT 5
Note values

The value of a note depends on its *shape*.

♩ is worth one beat and is called a crotchet.

♩ is worth two beats and is called a minim.

o is worth four beats and is called a semibreve.

Count four beats in a bar and see how these notes fit in with your counting.

Time signatures

There are two numbers written at the beginning of every piece of music. These numbers are called the time signature.

The top number tells you *how many* beats in a bar. The lower number tells you the *value* of each beat. If the lower number is 4, the beat is a crotchet. A $\frac{3}{4}$ time signature for example, will have three crotchet beats in each bar.

Repeat signs

If you want to play a piece or section of a piece over again, it is easier to use repeat signs. The signs look like this:

When you come to a repeat sign, go back to the beginning.

Repeat signs can be used in pairs. Instead of going back right to the beginning, go back only to the previous repeat sign.

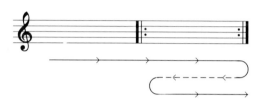

Repeat signs can have a 1st and a 2nd time bar. These two bars will be slightly different in chord and melody. Repeat from the first time bar, but on the second playing, you should miss out the first time bar and jump straight to the second time bar.

1. How many crotchet beats is Mr Note worth? Every shape is a note. (See page 40 for answer.)

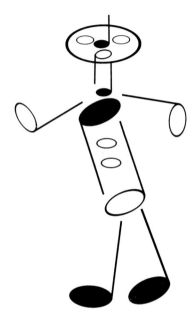

2. Play these rhythms on a note in the middle of the keyboard. Remember to count for each bar.

3. This exercise uses 1st and 2nd time bars. Choose a waltz rhythm at a moderate tempo. Press the synchro/start and you are ready to begin.

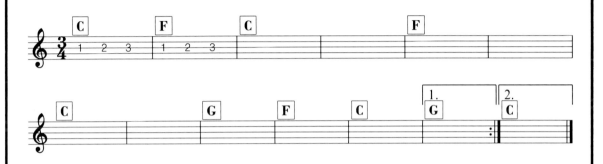

4. Here is a chord pattern which uses a pair of repeat signs. Choose a rock rhythm at a fast tempo. Press the synchro/start.

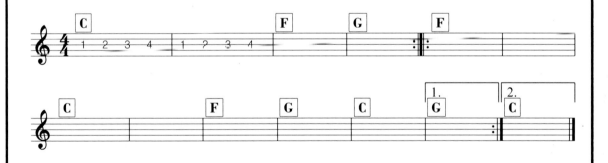

UNIT 6

Finding the notes

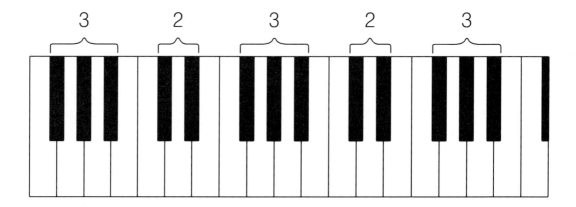

As you can see, the keyboard is made up of black and white keys. The black keys are laid out in alternate groups of twos and threes. It is these groups that tell you which notes are which.

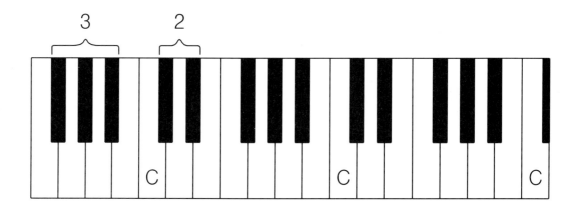

The white key to the left of the group of two black keys is called C. Find all the Cs on the keyboard.

You have found them because they are on the left of the group of two black keys. The white keys are named after the first seven letters of the alphabet: A–B–C–D–E–F–G. After G, the names of the notes start again with A. Find all the other white notes on the keyboard.

To start with, you will be using the notes in the middle of the keyboard to play melodies.

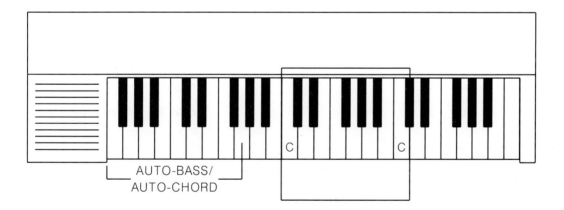

PROJECT WORK

1. Here is a jumbled-up list of letters from the musical alphabet. See how quickly you can find these on the keyboard: A, C, D, G, B, E, C, F, D, E, B, A, G, F, C.

2. You are going to have a 'musical' game of Scrabble. Using the letters A to G, play these words on the keyboard: BEEF, CABBAGE, AGE, EGG, BAGGAGE, FEED, ADDED.

3. See if you can play the following tunes. Use the keys in the middle of the keyboard.

Twinkle Twinkle Little Star

Frère Jacques

Unto us is born a Son

Blue Danube Waltz   Johann Strauss

UNIT 7
Starting to read music

Music is written on a set of five lines called a stave or staff. Each stave has five lines and four spaces. The notes can go on a line or in a space.

The symbol written at the beginning of the stave is called a clef. The clef which is usually used for melodies is called a treble clef or G clef. The note G is on the second line from the bottom.

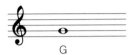

From this example you can work out the other notes.

The lower note C appears below the main stave and has a short line of its own. This note is called middle C. Find middle C on the keyboard.

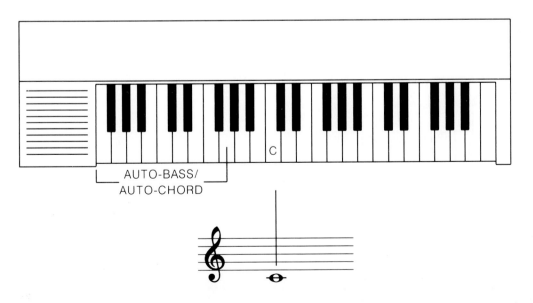

This note will be the starting point for the first few tunes. The tunes in this and the next unit will use only the five notes C, D, E, F, and G. Find them on your keyboard.

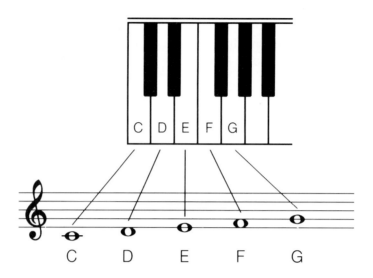

Fingering

The music will sound much smoother and more relaxed if you use all the fingers (including the thumb) to play the notes. Each finger is given a number which is shown above or below a selection of the notes.

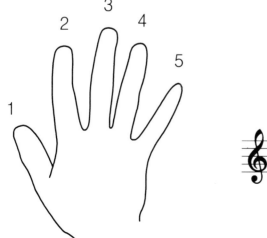

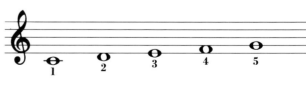

1. The letter names of the notes have been added to these two melodies. Try and read the actual notes rather than the letter names.

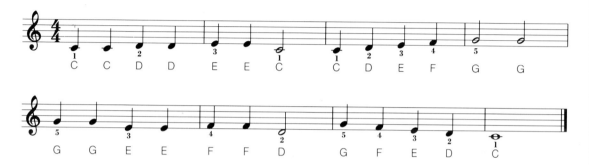

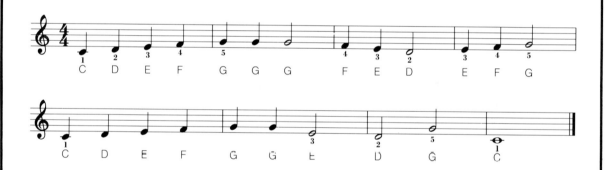

2. The following tunes use the notes C, D, E, F, and G. Place your fingers on these keys, and keep to the same fingering when you play the tunes.

SAILING

GLIDING

ROCKING

3. Here is the well-known melody *'Ode to Joy'* by Beethoven. It uses only crotchets, minims, and the notes C, D, E, F, and G.

'Ode to Joy' Beethoven

UNIT 8
Combining melody with chords

The left hand plays the chords on the auto-section of the keyboard, while the right hand plays the melody on the main part of the keyboard. Begin with practising chords and melody separately before attempting to play the parts together. Remember three things:

1. Each auto-chord key should be pressed only *once*. It will carry on repeating the chord until you press another key on the auto-section.

2. The melody note must be pressed down for its full value.

3. Do not confuse the chord letter with the melody note.

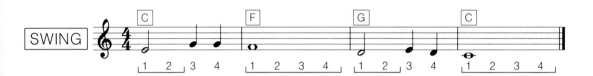

Some new signs

A minim with a dot written after it is called a dotted minim. It is worth three beats. A dot written after a note makes it longer by half its value.

If a note is joined to another note of the same pitch by a curved line, it is called a tied note.

The first note should be played and held on for the value of both notes. In the example, the total value of the note is five beats. The dotted minim has been 'stretched' into the next bar by another two beats.

The up-beat bar

Sometimes a song starts with an incomplete bar of music. This incomplete bar is called an up-beat. The missing beats are found in the last bar of the song. Do not press the auto-chord key until the first complete bar.

Playing louder and softer

p	*piano*	soft	*mp*	*mezzo piano*	moderately soft
f	*forte*	loud	*mf*	*mezzo forte*	moderately loud

◁ *crescendo (cresc)* gradually louder

◁ *diminuendo (dim)* gradually softer

PROJECT WORK

1. The famous tune *'Oh When the Saints go Marching in'* starts with an up-beat bar. Press the auto-chord key only when you have played the first three melody notes.

Oh When the Saints go Marching in

2. Here is a very simple melody with auto-chord accompaniment. Keep the melody note key pressed down for its full value. Each auto-chord key should be pressed only once. Choose an instrument which has a sustained tone, such as a violin or trumpet.

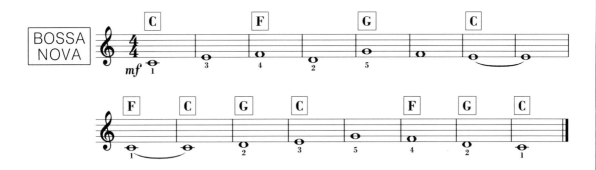

3. You have already played the melody *'Ode to Joy'* in Unit 7. This time, you are going to play it with the auto-chord accompaniment. Can you hear the difference? Some of the bars have two chords. Press the auto-chord key only on the first and third beats. It is here even more important to press the auto-chord key *exactly* on the right beat.

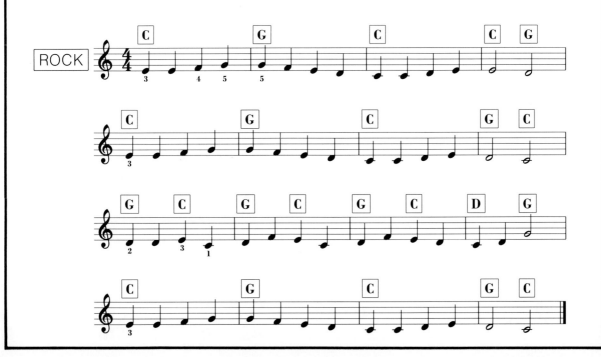

UNIT 9

Minor chords and the C major scale

A MINOR

Minor chords add variety to the music and can change the mood of the piece. Minor chords are shown by adding a small letter 'm' after the letter name of the chord: Am.

In order to play a minor chord, you need to press two keys *at the same time* on the auto-section of the keyboard. Here are two of the most usual ways of playing minor chords on the auto-section of the keyboard, but which method you use will depend on the make of the keyboard you play:

i) either play the letter name of the chord together with the black note to its *left* – diagram A;

or ii) play the letter name of the chord together with the white note to its *right* – diagram B.

Check with the keyboard manual to see which method you need to use.

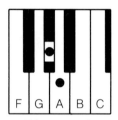

Diagram A

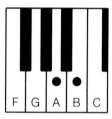

Diagram B

Some new notes

It is now time to add some more melody notes: A, B, C, D and E.

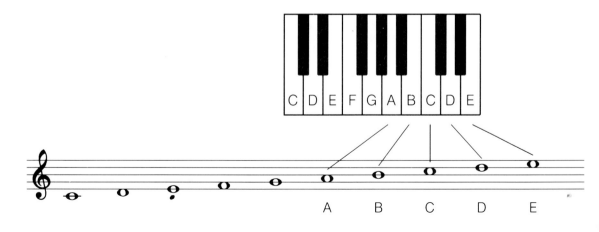

The distance between notes which have the same letter name is called an octave. (This word means an interval of eight notes.)

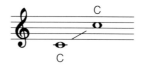

Scales

When all the other letter names are played in order between the octave, it is called a scale. Here is the scale of C major.

Play the scale with your right hand and practise the finger change until it is smooth and natural.

Note stems

The stems of notes can point up or down depending where they are on the stave. Below the middle line they point up, and above the middle line they point down. This makes the notes look tidy on the stave. Notes are either like the letter p (♪) or the letter d ( ); never ⌐ or ⌐ .

1. This chord pattern uses major and minor chords. Listen to the difference between the two types of chords. Remember to press the two keys on the auto-section *at the same time* for the minor chord pattern.

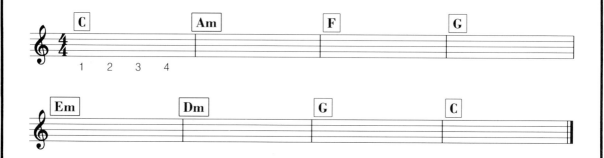

2. You will not have enough fingers for this melody without crossing your second finger over the thumb to play the note G. Use your thumb as a 'pivot' and your finger will go over quite naturally.

Canon   Johann Pachelbel

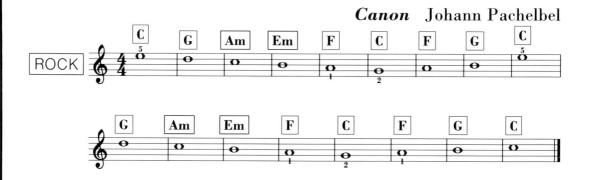

3. Make sure you play the minor chords correctly when you play the following two melodies.

The Skaters Waltz Emil Waldteufel

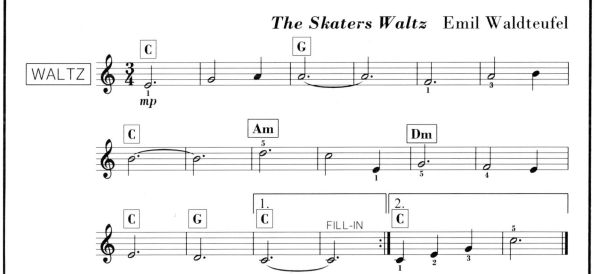

4.

Au Clair de la Lune French Trad.

UNIT 10
Quavers

Half beat notes are written with a 'tail' on
the stick. These notes are called quavers.
They are sometimes called 'eighth notes'
because there are eight quavers in a $\frac{4}{4}$ bar.

When the beat is a crotchet, the quavers
are usually grouped in pairs.

Pairs of quavers can be joined together in
each half of the bar.

See how quavers can fit into a rhythm
using all the note values you have played
so far.

Slurs

A curved line joining two or more different notes is called a slur. You should play them as smoothly as possible.

Staccato

If a dot is placed above or below a note, it should be played short and detached. This style of playing is called staccato.

Two more notes

Top F and G.

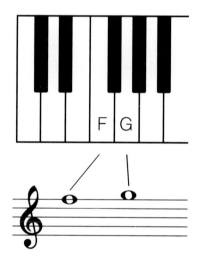

PROJECT WORK

1. Play these rhythms on the main keyboard . To help you keep time, use the auto-rhythm. The auto-chord should be switched off.

(a)

(b)

(c)

2. Keep counting crotchet beats in this melody. The auto-chord should be switched on.

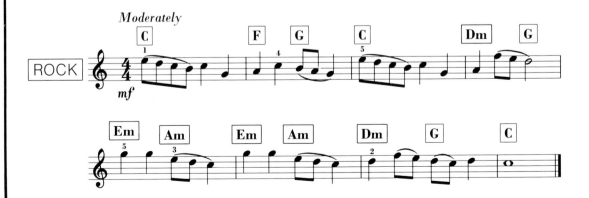

3. Use the volume control to give some contrast to this song.

Cradle Song Brahms

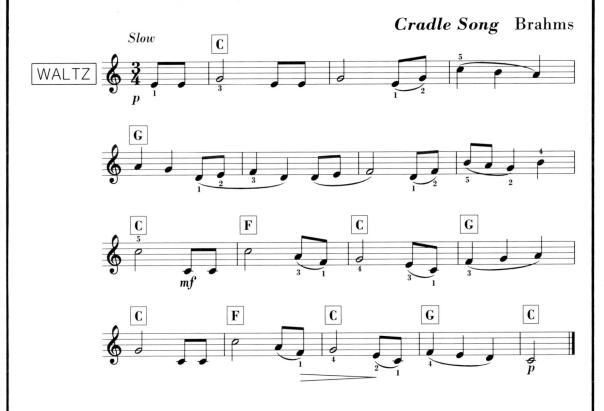

4. Move your fingers gently to slur the quavers.

The Ash Grove Welsh Trad.

UNIT 11
Dotted crotchets

A dot placed *after* a note lengthens it by half its own value. You have already used the dotted minim:

 = three beats

The dotted crotchet is worth one and a half beats.

 = one and a half beats

The dotted note is really a quicker and easier way of writing two notes joined with a tie. Play these two examples:

(a)

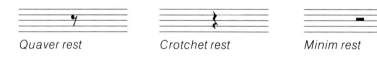

(b)

Both examples should sound exactly the same.

Rests

Rests are just as important as notes. A rest indicates a period of silence.

Quaver rest   *Crotchet rest*   *Minim rest*   *Semibreve rest or a whole bar's rest*

PROJECT WORK

1. Use the auto-rhythm to help you keep time with these rhythm exercises. The auto-chord should be switched off.

2. Keep strict time when you are playing the dotted notes in this piece.

Michael Row the Boat Ashore

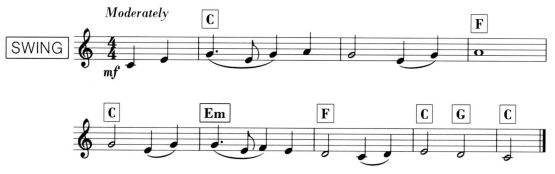

3. This famous melody is usually played by symphony orchestras and brass bands. Choose a woodwind instrument such as an oboe or clarinet. The auto-chord should be switched on.

Theme from 'The New World' Dvořák (arr. N. Haines)

Answer for page 18: Mr Note is worth 33 crotchets.